Making Portfolio Assessment Easy

Reproducible Forms and Checklists and Strategies for Using Them

MARY SULLIVAN

Scholastic

Scholastic Canada Ltd.
123 Newkirk Road, Richmond Hill, Ontario, Canada L4C 3G5

Scholastic Inc.
555 Broadway, New York, NY 10012-3999, USA

Ashton Scholastic Limited
Private Bag 92801, Penrose, Auckland, New Zealand

Ashton Scholastic Pty Limited
PO Box 579, Gosford, NSW 2250, Australia

Scholastic Publications Ltd.
Villiers House, Clarendon Avenue, Leamington Spa,
Warwickshire CV32 5PR, UK

Acknowledgments:

"Five Little Squirrels." Author unknown. From *Sing a Song of Popcorn: Every Child's Book of Poems*, selected by Beatrice Schenk de Regniers, Eva Moore, Mary Michaels White, and Jan Carr. Copyright © 1988 by Scholastic Inc. Reprinted by permission.

"The Mice and the Cat" by Aesop. From *Multicultural Fables and Fairy Tales* by Tara McCarthy. Copyright © 1993 by Tara McCarthy. Reprinted by permission.

ISBN: 0-590-24507-4

6 5 4 3 2 1   Printed in Canada   5 6 7 8 9/9

Contents

About Portfolio Assessment

Every day in our classrooms, we observe and think about what our students know and can do so that we can create the best possible environment for them to reach and grow. We use a variety of measures, both formal and informal, to document and reflect on their learning. Portfolio assessment is one such measure, one that enhances and broadens the way we look at learning performance. It encourages us to look at learning in the context of the whole child and to see performance as one facet of learning.

Often, it is useful to think of the portfolio as a literacy album with pictures representing the child's learning history, accomplishments, and growth.

- It documents individual student performances, attitudes, behaviors, and experiences.
- It collects information from teachers, families, and students using a variety of tools, including interviews, checklists, and demonstrations.
- It gathers samples of student work to aid teachers, families, and students themselves in assessing learning. In so doing, it provides a unique opportunity to collect the various stages of a piece of writing, from rough jot notes to polished, finished work.
- It empowers students. As students see their own progress, participate in evaluating their literacy development, and set literacy goals for themselves, they feel a heightened sense of control and self-esteem as language users.
- It invites a student's unique presentation of self.
- It facilitates communication with families and other educators. The detailed evidence, the samples and examples, and the opportunities to make comparisons with earlier demonstrations enhance the sharing of information in both interviews and formal reports.
- It encourages us to reflect on our own knowledge and on language learning in general. In examining the portfolios in our classrooms, we find reason to celebrate gains made by groups of children, and we discover the efficacy of particular teaching and learning strategies and materials.

By attending with care and sensitivity to what students experience, know, and can do, we are able to view their performance within the larger framework of the whole child and within the framework of literacy development. We are then able to predict the learning supports a child will need, both at school and at home. Dated samples of work, systematically collected and organized, give us a series of reference points that permit us to build on student strengths, address student needs, and help students themselves observe their development as learners. Such samples have meaning in and of themselves, unlike percentages, scores, and letter grades.

As we animate the portfolios through our choices, our practice, and our insights — as students color and shape them through their unique contributions — a profile of each emerging language user will unfold.

Managing Portfolio Assessment

The portfolio is a place for teachers to gather and preserve assessment information about student literacy development. For that reason, if space permits, it should remain in the school for as long as the learner attends and should be available for the child to review, for the family to examine and discuss, and for other educators who work with the child to consult.

For portfolio assessment to be successful, all its participants must be clear about its purpose and uses. To students, you might present the metaphor of the literacy album, each of whose entries shows what they know and can do. Working with them to establish criteria for selecting and evaluating work for the portfolio establishes ownership in the process and helps them extend their understanding of what makes a good piece of writing. To families, you might send a note explaining portfolio assessment and soliciting their support and participation. To colleagues, you might say that you are implementing portfolio assessment in your classroom and invite them to observe the process — or join you in it. As a teacher, you will want to select items for the portfolio that meet your instructional and reporting needs. At first, you may wish to write portfolio assessment into your program plan to make sure you find time for it and so that its implementation supports your overall evaluation and reporting schedules.

Implementing portfolio assessment does require both time and planning: for face-to-face interaction with individual students or small groups of students; for the involvement of readers and scribes; and for discussion of portfolios with students and their families.

Getting Started

Before school begins, take some time to decide what each portfolio should include. The kinds of information and samples you collect will depend on how you identify and address learner strengths and needs; how you develop and assess your classroom curriculum; and what you are mandated to assess formally. Portfolio assessment should support all of these purposes.

Establish a convenient place in the classroom for the portfolios, and gather the materials for them. Two possibilities are legal-size file folders and large sheets of construction paper, which the children can use to make folders.

During the first week of school, acquaint families with portfolio assessment. In a meeting or in a note, explain the process to them and solicit their support. If you can, provide samples of portfolios so that they can see that portfolio assessment is a powerful and revealing assessment device. Let them know what they can do to assist with your portfolio program in the classroom and to promote their child's literacy at home. Begin to develop a literacy profile of each learner based on information from the family.

Collecting Baseline Samples

At the beginning of the school year, collect baseline or benchmark surveys and samples against which you can measure the child's literacy development. What you gather will depend upon what you will want to assess during the school year and upon the diagnostic evaluation tools you would normally use, but some possibilities include the following:

- fiction or non-fiction writing sample, in which you can observe the learner's imaginative capacity, ability to construct a piece of writing, knowledge of sequence, control of mechanics and vocabulary, and familiarity with conventions of spelling, punctuation, and letter formation
- record of reading fluency (including an audiotape, if appropriate)
- sample of sight words with which the learner is familiar
- checklist or survey of the learner's views about literacy and learning goals for the year
- information about family goals and expectations for the learner and a record of the learner's previous literacy experiences

Building the Portfolio

Throughout the year, each learner's literacy profile will unfold as dated items are added to the portfolio:

- samples that mark significant moments in the child's learning
- book logs showing what the learner has read
- multiple drafts of pieces of writing
- record(s) of reading fluency demonstrating increasing control of strategies and ability to deal with progressively more difficult texts
- growing lists of sight words and personal spelling lists
- assessments by the learner of work in the classroom and of what has been learned
- follow-up surveys of the child's views of literacy and learning

- new literacy goals that build on those the learner has met
- other diagnostic and formative evaluation tools that are important to your teaching practice
- other supports for your school's reporting system

The number and type of additions to the portfolio will depend upon the time available to you and on your own and your students' needs and strengths. Try to include in the portfolio significant markers or highlights of the child's literacy development. The timing of the additions should reflect your school's evaluation and reporting schedules.

At Year-End

With portfolios, assessment and evaluation are integrated and ongoing in the classroom. Nevertheless, the end of the school year invites particular reflection on what a child has accomplished and learned, on goals that have been achieved, and on planning for the year to come. Toward the end of the year, you will want to gather such information and samples as:

- final examples of student work, for comparison with the baseline samples
- record of reading fluency, for comparison with the baseline sample
- representative list of sight words and a personal spelling list
- checklist or survey reflecting the child's perception of what has been learned during the year
- information about the family's thoughts and feeling about the child's literacy development during the year
- summative evaluation to satisfy your reporting requirements

Professional References

Calkins, L. (1987). *The writing workshop — a world of difference: A guide for staff development.* Portsmouth, NH: Heinemann.

Clay, M. (1982). *Observing young readers.* Auckland, NZ: Heinemann.

Clay, M. (1975). *What did I write?* Auckland, NZ: Heinemann.

Clemmons, J., Laase, L., Cooper, D., Areglado, N., & Dill, M. (1993). *Portfolios in the classroom: A teacher's sourcebook.* NY: Scholastic.

Cooper, W., & Brown, B. (1992). Using portfolios to empower student writers. *English Journal, 81* (2), 40-45.

De Fina, Allan A. (1992). *Portfolio assessment: Getting started.* NY: Scholastic.

Goodman, Y., & Burke, C. (1970). *Reading miscue inventory.* Newark, DE: International Reading Association.

Holdaway, D. (1979). *The foundations of literacy.* Sydney: Ashton Scholastic.

Paulson, F., Paulson, P., & Meyer, C. (1991). What makes a portfolio a portfolio? *Educational Leadership, 48* (5), 60-63.

Picciotto, L. (1992). *Evaluation: A team effort.* Richmond Hill, ON: Scholastic Canada.

Powell, D., & Hornsby, D. (1993). *Learning phonics and spelling in a whole language classroom.* NY: Scholastic.

Valencia, S. (1990). A portfolio approach to classroom reading assessment: The whys, whats, and hows. *The Reading Teacher, 43* (4), 338-340.

Yancey, K. (Ed.). (1992). *Portfolios in the writing classroom: An introduction.* Urbana, IL: National Council of Teachers of English.

Getting Started

At the beginning of the school year, inform and advise parents about portfolio assessment. Collect baseline or benchmark samples or surveys against which learning can be measured. Introduce **Books I Have Read** and begin to keep anecdotal records on each child using **Worthy of Note** or another system that you find useful.

#	Page	Date	Date
1	In this Portfolio		
2	Continuum of Knowledge, Skills, and Attitudes		
3	Continuum of Knowledge, Skills, and Attitudes		
4	About Portfolios		
5	My Name Is		
6	Interview		
7	Personal Inventory		
8	A Note from Home		
9	Record of Reading Fluency		
10	Impromptu Writing Sample		
11	Book Knowledge Checklist		
12	Spelling Diagnosis		
13	Spelling Sight Words		
14	Punctuation Knowledge		
15	Books I Have Read		
16	Worthy of Note		

In this Portfolio

Throughout the year, you will be collecting samples and examples that demonstrate the learner's understandings and attitudes about literacy and progression along the learning continuum in all literacy domains. Use this page to:

- keep track of what is in the portfolio
- assist in goal-setting for learning
- plan for instruction and future assessment

Review this checklist (**Reproducible 1**) periodically to ensure that the portfolio you are building accurately portrays the child's abilities and reveals the child's needs. You can also use it to record the kinds of artifacts you are collecting to ensure a balance in all literacy domains and areas of the curriculum and to ensure that the portfolio will support the reporting scheme in your school.

Continuum of Knowledge, Skills, and Attitudes

Key to portfolio assessment is the belief that children's literacy learning proceeds at different rates and at different times along a continuum from novice to mature language user. Many facets of such learning are set out in the continuum of literacy development (**Reproducibles 2** and **3**). The aspects of literacy learning set out on these pages are not sequenced, but overall, there is a movement toward a broader scope of language knowledge and ability and an increased sophistication in literacy.

You may find the continuum useful as a diagnostic tool as you plan the curriculum in your classroom. You may also wish to share these pages with families as you explain how you will use portfolio assessment to track the learning of their children.

In this Portfolio

On this page, record items added to the portfolio.

Also use it to highlight particular aspects of a child's work.

Notes:

Date	Item	Comments

Date: _____ **◆ I** Name: _____

Knowledge

The student knows:

that books contain stories
that print represents thought and speech
that print goes from left to right / top to bottom of the page
some letter names

that words are clusters of letters with spaces between them
some high-frequency words
there is a sound-symbol relationship
parts of book (such as *title, pages, dedication*)

Reading / Thinking Development
Skills
The student is able to:

role-play reading
handle books appropriately
retell stories
make predictions from illustrations
anticipate pattern repetitions

recognize some words
make connections between letters / letter clusters and
  sounds
read many words using a variety of strategies

Attitudes / Behaviors
The student:

enjoys listening to stories
likes to look through books
thinks of self as reader
notices print in the environment
handles books appropriately
wants to see the print when read to

asks for certain stories
talks about books
selects books independently
uses a variety of strategies to make sense of print
enjoys and repeats rhymes and patterns from books
retells stories without prompting

Writing / Thinking Development
Semantic Skills
The student is able to:

generate material for writing
create simple narration
write several sequenced events
create simple description
elaborate with detail

write for a sustained period of time
generate imaginative and original material
use strong nouns and strong verbs
create a main impression or make a point
copy patterns of rhythm and rhyme

Syntactic Skills
The student is able to:

use scribble writing
form some letters and numbers
copy letters and words
form letters recognizably
represent some sounds by letter

separate letter clusters to represent words
use basic punctuation
produce some sight words correctly
represent many sounds correctly
generate readable prose

Attitudes / Behaviors
The student:

engages in writing as a self-initiated activity
writes willingly when asked to do so
sustains interest in a writing task
is willing to share writing with others
is interested in the writing of others

chooses topics readily
generates ideas freely
risks spelling unknown words
uses many strategies for attempting and checking spelling
seeks verification of spelling after writing

Skills, and Attitudes

Knowledge

The student knows:

some of the purposes of print
that people read for many purposes
many sight words
many sound-sight correlations of letters and groups of letters

function of punctuation and capital letters
the elements of story
some literary terminology
names and characteristics of various genres

Reading / Thinking Development
Skills

The student is able to:

extract general meaning from a text
comprehend what is read
make inferences
bring personal response to literature
see cause and effect

distinguish between fact and fiction
distinguish between fact and opinion
discern the purpose of a piece of writing
identify main points and supporting information

Attitudes / Behaviors
The student:

takes books home from school
shares books with others
thinks of self as reader
reads at home
becomes engrossed in print / story
reads print in the environment

explores books, magazines in library
notices novelty in words, stories, graphics
explores many genres, styles, authors
tackles books above the level of easy reading
uses the library
reads regularly for pleasure and to find information

Writing / Thinking Development
Semantic Skills

The student is able to:

use figurative language
discuss the writing process
understand the purpose of revision
rearrange, change, and edit work
write with sophistication equal to speaking ability

use patterns or conventions from literature
write for many purposes
write narrative, descriptive, and expository material with
   confidence and competence
use various strategies to generate material for writing

Syntactic Skills
The student is able to:

consistently spell many words correctly
use strategies for figuring out possible spellings of
   unfamiliar words
print or write legibly
use punctuation and capital letters correctly

spell most words correctly or sensibly
identify possible misspellings
express ideas and share information through a variety of
   formats and genres
organize material coherently and sequentially

Attitudes / Behaviors
The student:

rereads work while writing
adds details
seeks response of others to work
reflects on aspects of own compositions
discusses work of other writers

imitates patterns, styles, and techniques of other writers
willingly invests in reshaping and revising work
has standards for personal written work
seeks to share, publish, display writing
writes for many purposes

About Portfolios

Implementing a portfolio program requires the support and commitment of all its participants: the learners in your class, their families, and your colleagues.

Before you begin, read up on portfolio assessment and talk to your colleagues and administrators about implementing it.

Then, you will need to decide what kinds of materials you will be collecting in the portfolio. In your first year of implementation, you may need to be selective in the kinds of pieces you gather so that you can gauge the amount of time portfolio assessment will take and the amount of family support you can expect.

Your next step will be to inform families and involve them in your portfolio program. The letter on this page is an introduction, but you may also wish to discuss portfolio assessment in a meeting with the family at the beginning of the school year. At the same time, you can suggest ways in which families can participate in your program. Encourage them to help determine what should be collected and also to work as scribes or mentors in the program. You might also discuss how families can support their children's literacy in the home. Time and planning are keys to the success of your portfolio assessment program.

Use or adapt the letter to suit your purposes and your classroom.

About Portfolios

Dear Parent:

Just like you, I want to make sure that your child is able to make the best possible use of this school year. One of the tools I will be using to check on your child's learning is portfolio assessment.

Throughout the year, your child and I will select and insert materials into the portfolio. I will be choosing and commenting on pieces that show how your child's learning is unfolding. Your child will also be selecting works for the portfolio. As we talk about reasons for choosing particular works, your child will further develop abilities to think critically and solve problems. At the same time, I will have a better understanding of your child's thoughts and values.

In the portfolio, I will also be saving checklists and your child's own assessments of reading and writing, as well as notes from you about your child's learning.

When you look through your child's portfolio, you will be able to see at a glance how your child is developing as a reader, writer, and thinker.

Would you like to help? If you can give me some of your time, please fill in the bottom of this page and return it to me. But even if you can't help out, you are welcome to chat with me about your child's learning — and see your child's portfolio — anytime.

❏   Yes, I can help with the portfolio program at school.

❏   No, I can't help out at school, but I'll help my child at home.

Name: _____   My Child's Name: _____

Phone: _____

My Name Is

As the learner personalizes this page, you will have an early indication of writing ability. The child may be able to form only a few letters and perhaps remember a sequence, or he or she may be able to write fluently. As the child writes and draws, you will also gain a sense of the child's attitude and persistence in responding to a task.

From time to time throughout the year, remind your students why they should not erase their early writing efforts. You might draw a parallel between the portfolio and a literacy album or compare looking at the portfolio with admiring a baby picture: "We can see how you've grown and changed." Every time they look back at this page, they will be able to see for themselves how much they have grown as writers and thinkers. Throughout the year, you will be able to celebrate learning with the children.

My Name Is

The student prints his or her name independently and then personalizes the page by writing or drawing.

Observe:

☐ ability to form letters
☐ fluency in writing
☐ attentiveness to task
☐

Notes:

My portfolio shows some of the things I can do.

Date: _____   **5**   Name: _____

Interview

To design appropriate supports in the classroom, we need information about the learner's self-concept as a productive member of the learning community and as a capable person in the home environment. The more we know about the whole child, the more informed we will be in our design of such supports. Knowing something about the student's self-perception as a learner or as a helper at home helps us to know where to intervene and how to encourage development of positive self-concept.

Interviews are one way to discover such information. As well, interviews encourage students to present themselves as individuals who already have a history of successful learning and doing.

Plan to interview a child at least once during each reporting period of the school year. Follow-up interviews encourage learners to reflect on their experiences at school, to evaluate personal performance against previous personal performance and against the performance of others, and to set new learning goals for themselves. For you, interviews may provide clues and context to learning.

In a conversation with the student, elicit and record the information on the page.

Notes:

Interview

Things I like about myself:

_____

_____

_____

_____

What I think about school:

_____

_____

_____

_____

What I hope to learn this year:

_____

_____

_____

_____

How I can learn to do this:

_____

_____

_____

_____

Date: _____   ◆ 6 ◆   Name: _____

Personal Inventory

Knowing what learners like to do when they are in charge of their own time tells us a great deal about them. The knowledge we have about student strengths, values, and interests helps us to understand them, motivate them, and open up possibilities for them.

In an individual conference, let the child talk about interests, likes, and dislikes, and fill in the page accordingly.

Use this page at the beginning of the school year. You may wish to use it on one or more additional occasions during the school year to refocus attention on a learner's knowledge and interests.

Discuss the page in individual conference. Then scribe responses, or have the student complete the page independently.

Observe student:

❑ interests
❑ preferences
❑ strengths
❑

Notes:

Personal Inventory

Some things I can do well:

_____

_____

_____

Some things that interest me:

_____

_____

_____

Some things I would like to know more about:

_____

_____

_____

Some things I think are great:

_____

_____

_____

Some things I don't like much:

_____

_____

_____

Date: _____ **7** Name: _____

A Note from Home

We know that rich exposure to all manner of language experience, including extensive experience with print and story, puts some beginning readers light years ahead of those who have not had such experience. Out-of-school reading, family models, and motivation to read are all important aspects of literacy development.

Having information about this critical "hidden foundation" for learning is invaluable as we design appropriate support structures for the growth of young readers. Also important is information about the learner's reading patterns, preferences, attitudes, and self-perceptions. As teachers, we want to know the interests of our students, the kinds of books they read, the amount of reading they do, and the circumstances that enhance reading for them.

Use this page to gather information about the learner's literacy experiences outside the classroom. You can also use it to record family expectations for the child. Encourage families to take a few minutes to fill in the page when they register their child for school. If this is not possible, you might send the form home with the student or discuss it with the child's family during an interview or over the telephone. As the learner meets parental goals during the course of the year, you can encourage him or her to set new learning goals in consultation with you and the family.

The page will be useful for follow-up interviews with both student and family.

A Note from Home

Your knowledge about your child and your observations throughout the year are important and can assist me significantly in meeting your child's needs. Please return this form to me, and I will place it in your child's learning portfolio.

Please describe your child's:

interest in books, magazines, newspapers _____

_____

interest in reading with you or another relative, or with a friend _____

_____

interest in writing _____

_____

attitude toward school subjects and school activities _____

_____

relationships with family members and friends _____

_____

hobbies and interests _____

_____

hopes and fears for school _____

_____

Please comment on your goals for your child this year. _____

_____

_____

_____

Date: _____   Name: _____

Record of Reading Fluency

Miscue analysis, developed by Yetta M. Goodman and Carolyn L. Burke (1970), assists teachers in observing and recording reading behaviors. Use miscue analysis to assess the learner's ability to do the following: make graphophonic connections; use strategies and cuing systems to construct meaning from print; comprehend and analyze information presented in text; and show understanding of what has been read.

Choose a text that challenges the learner's independent reading level. It may be necessary to experiment with several books until you find a sufficiently challenging text, one that allows observation of how the child makes sense of print. Have the child read the text, and tape the oral reading. Wherever a child's reading differs from the printed text, mark up a copy of the text using the symbols that follow.

Substitutes:	Write substitute word(s) above line
Self-corrects:	
successfully	Write (SC) above the correction
unsuccessfully	Write (UC) above the correction
Omits:	Circle word(s) or punctuation omitted
Inserts:	Use caret (∧) and write inserted word
Reverses:	Use transposition mark (book the) around words
Repeats:	Underline repeated text

Discuss the text after the reading. Encourage the child to make inferences and personal connections to the text. You may also wish to have the child retell the story as a comprehension check.

As you review the taped reading, consider whether the reader's miscues affected meaning and how and why the reader self-corrected. From the *kinds* of miscues, you will be able to tell which reading strategies and cuing systems your students are using and which are not yet in their repertoire. From the *number* of miscues, you can make inferences about appropriate kinds and levels of reading materials.

Use this page as often as necessary throughout the school year to document the child's increasing ability to deal with different kinds of print materials of differing levels of difficulty.

Record of Reading Fluency

Choose a reading selection of appropriate difficulty. The student reads from the book while you record miscues and strategies used.

So that you can observe the strategies used, you may need to have the student attempt several pieces until reading fluency decreases.

An oral retelling of the story is a useful comprehension check.

Observe:

❏ plot events and sequence recalled
❏ understanding of cause and effect
❏ characters and relationships recalled
❏ inferences made
❏ setting recalled
❏ use of description
❏

If selection is expository...

❏ main idea recalled
❏ general concepts understood
❏ detail recalled
❏ logical structuring

Notes:

Title of selection(s):

Miscue summary
   with no meaning loss (*type, number, and comments*)

   with meaning loss (*type, number, and comments*)

Reading strategies / cuing systems
   in place

   to be introduced

Comments on student retelling:

Student questions, perception of self as reader:

Date: _____   **9**   Name: _____

Impromptu Writing Sample

As learners write, they compose mentally, generate print, and reshape the writing to create an original text. Collecting and analyzing successive stages of the same piece of writing — both draft and polished text — allows us to observe the child's thought processes, attentiveness to both content and structure of language, and willingness and ability to revise. The samples provide evidence of written language development, and you can use them in planning your programming.

Collect several impromptu writing samples over the course of the year to provide a full picture of the learner's progression along the literacy continuum and to support your school's reporting schedule. In selecting pieces, look for successive drafts that demonstrate how the child is internalizing the process of writing.

Impromptu Writing Sample

Collect for the portfolio all drafts of a piece of writing, from brainstorming notes to finished product.

Observe:

- ☐ sources of ideas
- ☐ understanding of directionality of print, letters, spaces, numbers
- ☐ description, detail, elaboration
- ☐ sequenced narration
- ☐ organization of ideas
- ☐ use of humor
- ☐ vocabulary usage
- ☐ spelling strategies in place
- ☐ use of final punctuation
- ☐ use of capital letters
- ☐ printing or handwriting
- ☐

Notes:

Why you chose this piece of writing:

Changes from first to final draft:

Writing strategies in place:

Writing strategies that need work:

Student comments on the process of creating this piece:

Date: _____
Name: _____

Book Knowledge Checklist

Early in the school year, establish a baseline measure against which a learner's familiarity with print, with books, with story, and with literary vocabulary can be gauged.

If children have had limited exposure to books, you may want to use prompts such as the following:

"What is this?" [*Show the book.*] "What is it for?" "Can you show me ...?" "How would you ...?" " What do you think ...?"

For children with more experience, initiate a conversation about books. Have the child use a book to demonstrate knowledge: what books are, what people do with them, what readers can find in them, and so on. Some children will show and tell everything you want to know with little prompting. Others will need you to probe for every response. Encourage the child to speculate on what the book is about, and record how the predictions are made.

This checklist is useful for diagnostic purposes. It is also easily understood by students. Whenever they look back at it, they will be able to see for themselves how much they have learned about reading — and how they are maturing as readers.

Plan to use this page once in each reporting period of the school year.

Book Knowledge Checklist

Use one or more books of various types (fiction, non-fiction, poetry) to initiate a conversation about books.

As the student speaks, observe his or her handling of the book.

Probe for use and understanding of such terms as *author, glossary,* and *index.*

Notes:

	YES •	NOT YET
I know what books are.	❏	❏
I know why people use books.	❏	❏
I know what a title is.	❏	❏
I know what an author is.	❏	❏
I know what an illustrator is.	❏	❏
I know how to hold a book.	❏	❏
I know where to start reading.	❏	❏
I know where to go when I reach the end of the page.	❏	❏
I know where to find the end of the book.	❏	❏
I know how to use captions.	❏	❏
I know how to use an index and a glossary.	❏	❏

Other things I know about books:

_____

_____

Date: _____ ◆ **11** Name: _____

Spelling Diagnosis

By observing children's spellings, we are able to assess the intervention they need to expand their repertoire and gain competence in this aspect of their development as emerging writers. Some spellings can be arrived at through problem-solving with a knowledge of English phonetic patterns. Other words do not follow phonetic patterns and are learned as memorized letter groupings or "sight words." This page deals with the first group.

By analyzing children's attempts to spell these words, we are able to recognize graphophonic matches that are in line with possible English spellings. If a child spells *surfing* as *surphing*, we see that he or she knows that *ph* can represent the *f* sound in English. We might see that certain letters are consistently substituted for others. It is possible that the letters in question are mispronounced by the child. Perhaps there are reversals or omissions that can point to specific areas of difficulty or confusion.

A learner's spelling can be observed through analysis of written work, through dictated text, or through presentation of selected words. The following lists present some representations of the early challenges students will encounter as they begin to make graphophonic connections. Where words are given from the list, it is best to observe the learner in a one-on-one performance. Use discretion with regard to the number of words administered in one sitting. Present each word in the context of a sentence or phrase. Because this is a diagnostic tool, focus on the description and analysis of the child's spelling rather than on the number of errors. Collect a baseline sample to determine the graphophonic matches under control by the learner and those still requiring reinforcement through reading and shared writing, through display and direct teaching. Depending on your purpose, you can collect the same or different words in later samples.

List 1: mom, dad, pet, stop, run, name, green, climb, home, soon, star, work
List 2: fix, dinner, going, then, what, chin, push, fast, boy, girl, turn, here
List 3: bottle, ice, age, quick, best, tub, love, stuff, night, laugh, photo, write
List 4: high, know, hair, talk, baby, played, shout, long, robin, call, bath
List 5: much, sink, swim, late, silly, tries, answer, until, listen, hold, salt
List 6: happy, toys, glue, mail, seed, coat, walked, few, crow, meat, say, pie
List 7: shoes, store, glad, brave, grow, sign, skip, stream, spy, scar, bookshelf
List 8: daughter, right, question, beginning, playground, grandparents
List 9: *words from reading and writing in your classroom*

Spelling Diagnosis

Select words of appropriate difficulty and present them in the context of a sentence or phrase.

Concepts (check all appropriate):

- ☐ short vowel sounds
- ☐ long vowel sounds
- ☐ vowel in every syllable
- ☐ initial consonants
- ☐ final consonants
- ☐ blends: st/cl/gr/sw ...
- ☐ digraphs: ck/nk/ng/ch/sh ...
- ☐ silent letters
- ☐ common suffixes/ inflections: ed/ing
- ☐ "gh," "ph" understood as "f"
- ☐ plural form: "ies"
- ☐
- ☐

Strategies in place:
- ☐
- ☐
- ☐

Notes:

_____

_____

_____

_____

_____

_____

_____

_____

_____

_____

_____

_____

_____

Student comments on spelling:

_____

_____

Date: _____   Name: _____

Spelling Sight Words

Many words in our language do not follow phonetic patterns. Some have irregularities which make them difficult or impossible to spell by a problem-solving or "sounding out" approach. Here, teachers will be interested in a baseline sample that shows percentage of sight words under control, as well as parts of words spelled correctly. Repeating the task at other times of the year will help to indicate the gains being made by learners as they are exposed to reading and writing activities and to instruction.

For these types of words it is important to talk to children about strategies for memorizing or remembering words by association, by linking them to known words or parts of words, by noticing irregularities, by chanting letter sequence, and so on.

The words that follow are drawn from lists of high-frequency words in print and in children's writing. These are sight words that students will begin to recognize during the primary grades through their reading and writing, as well as through direct teaching. The lists will accommodate a diversity of levels of spelling ability in your classroom, but you should also add words from children's experiences in the classroom. Select only the level and number of words that can be comfortably handled at one time, and present each word in the context of a sentence or phrase.

List 1: man, about, some, your, now, long, said, very, which, one
List 2: other, around, made, each, first, woman, them, time, what, there
List 3: could, house, because, their, use, before, does, been, want, over
List 4: would, much, how, two, people, her, him, make, his, were, here
List 5: friend, country, school, video, movies, soccer, canoe, tomorrow, bicycle, beautiful
List 6: across, writing, interesting, telephone, visiting, Monday, Tuesday, Wednesday, Thursday, Friday
List 7: September, October, November, December, January, February, March, April, *your town/city/school name*

Because this is a diagnostic tool, no attempt should be made to drill students on the words or to prepare them in any way.

Collect the baseline sample, and then gather additional samples throughout the year as you require to observe the growth in the student's sight word vocabulary.

Spelling Sight Words

Select words of appropriate difficulty and present them in the context of a sentence or phrase.

Graphophonic matches:

☐
☐
☐
☐

Notes:

_____

_____

_____

_____

_____

_____

_____

_____

_____

_____

_____

Student comments on spelling:

_____

_____

Date: _____   **13**   Name: _____

Punctuation Knowledge

As learners become more familiar with reading, they notice punctuation and use such print signals to help them build meaning. Punctuation creeps into their writing (or explodes, at times — as learners use periods after every word, for instance!).

Writing samples in the portfolio will reveal the student's growing awareness of punctuation, as well as usage that is increasingly conventional. You may wish to have the student evaluate the use of punctuation in his or her own writing.

This page provides an opportunity to record the student's recognition and understanding of print conventions. Use the poem, or select another suitable piece of writing. Once the student is familiar with the piece, draw attention to the punctuation marks and print signals. Have the learner identify them and discuss their purpose.

Collect the baseline sample, and then plan to use the page again at the end of the school year, or more often as your reporting schedule dictates.

Punctuation Knowledge

Point to each print signal, and ask the student to explain its purpose.

You may prefer to use a different piece of writing.

Student:
- ❏ names quotation marks
- ❏ knows their purpose

- ❏ names comma
- ❏ knows its purpose

- ❏ names period
- ❏ knows its purpose

- ❏ names exclamation mark
- ❏ knows its purpose

- ❏ names apostrophe
- ❏ knows its purpose

- ❏ understands why "I'm" is italicized

- ❏ understands why "BANG" is capitalized

- ❏ names exclamation mark
- ❏ knows its purpose

- ❏
- ❏

Notes:

Five Little Squirrels

Five little squirrels
Sat in a tree.
The first one said,
"What do I see?"
The second one said,
"A man with a gun."
The third one said,
"We'd better run."
The fourth one said,
"Let's hide in the shade."
The fifth one said,
"*I'm* not afraid."
Then BANG went the gun,
And how they did run!

Author Unknown

Student comments on punctuation knowledge:

_____

_____

_____

_____

Date: _____ **14** Name: _____

Books I Have Read

Since we know that "learning how to read" and "becoming a reader" are two different things, we want to know about the reading patterns of young readers in order to encourage in them the development of the "reading habit."

Keeping a book log allows learners to see themselves as readers. Making evaluative comments helps them begin to develop a critical appreciation of books. You will be able to see the number and type of books being read, which will help you select topics and books for reading and discussing with the child. You will also be able to monitor whether a child needs to be nudged in the direction of books of a different type or length or level.

Store the reading logs in an accessible place in the classroom, and have the children record all their reading choices, including such materials as magazine articles or comic books. Solicit the help of parents or librarians to keep the list current. The copy of the log filed in the portfolio will be a permanent record of the learner's reading patterns, preferences, and increasing sophistication as a reader.

Consider keeping your own book log so that children can observe the kinds of comments you record.

Books I Have Read

Title	Author	Date	Comments

Name: _____

Date: _____

Worthy of Note

You may wish to reproduce a copy of this page for each child in your class. File the pages in a binder, and use them to record dated general comments and anecdotal observations. Once you have filled the pages, you can transfer them to the portfolio. Your anecdotal comments will be helpful in verbal or written reports to parents or other educators.

Use this page as often as necessary during the school year to provide a complete picture of the child's development in all domains.

Record general observations, and comment on particular moments that reveal significant learning or behaviors.

Date each observation to show the child's development as a learner.

Areas might include any of the following:

- ❐ classroom participation
- ❐ social interactions
- ❐ leadership
- ❐ student questioning
- ❐ problem-solving
- ❐ work habits
- ❐ creativity
- ❐ responsibility for materials/space
- ❐ attitudes
- ❐ attendance
- ❐ health concerns

- ❐
- ❐

Worthy of Note

Building the Portfolio

Choose whichever of the following you need to meet the objectives you have established for your portfolio program. Samples and surveys can be collected in any sequence. To provide for a full picture of a child's learning development, you may need to collect more than one example of some of the elements.

#	Page	Date	Date
17	Participation and Responsibility		
18	Letter Names		
19	Consonant and Vowel Sounds		
20	Consonant Combinations		
21	Diphthongs and Digraphs		
22	Story Structure		
23	Understanding Information		
24	Responding to Literature		
25	Tell Me a Story		
26	My Talk Checklist		
27	Listening and Speaking		
28	Student Talk		
29	Color Words		
30	Reading Directions		
31	Following Directions		
32	Searching for Information		

#	Page	Date	Date
33	Understanding Print		
34	Story Mapping		
35	Making Inferences		
36	Identifying Problems		
37	Responding to Poetry		
38	My Reading Checklist		
39	Thoughts About Reading		
40	About Literature		
41	Selected Work		
42	Information Writing		
43	Writing a Sequel		
44	About Writing		
45	About Revising		
46	Writing and Editing		
47	My Writing Checklist		
48	Before I Write		
49	While I'm Writing		
50	Changing My Work		
51	How I Spell		
52	Dictation		
53	Best Printing or Writing		
54	My Handwriting Checklist		

Also consider revisiting and updating some of the pages you collected at the beginning of the school year: **Reproducibles 6, 9, 10, 11, 12, 13, and 15.**

Participation and Responsibility

Knowing something about how the learner perceives himself or herself as a member of the learning community or as a helper at home helps us to know when to intervene and how to encourage the development of positive self-concept.

Read each statement with the child, and invite a response. The page provides an opportunity to discuss the child's attitude toward learning.

You may wish to add your own perception of student participation and responsibility.

Plan to use this page in each reporting period during the school year.

Read each statement with the student and record his or her responses.

Have the student set goals for participation and responsibility.

Notes:

	Most of the time	Some-times	Hardly Ever	Not Yet
I listen to the teacher and to other students when they read or speak.				
I start my work right away.				
I give my ideas and offer answers to questions.				
I try to figure things out for myself when I am given a job.				
I ask for help when I need it.				
I help others if I see they need help or if they ask.				
I am nice to other students.				
I let other students play in my games and with my toys.				
I put things back where they belong.				
I remember to take home papers and forms.				

What I would like to do better:

_____

_____

_____

How I can do this better:

_____

_____

_____

Date: _____ **17** Name: _____

Letter Names

As we work with children to mediate the world of print, we need the language of letter names at times to talk about sound-symbol matching. Certainly it is possible for children to learn to read without knowing the names of letters; however, since school is about trying to maximize opportunities for learning, and precision of language is a key enhancer of that learning, it makes sense for us to give children that language.

This page reveals the learner's knowledge of two basic conventions of print: letter names and their capital and lower-case forms. Point to the letters in any order, and circle those correctly named.

Use this page with emergent readers as often as necessary to provide a record of the child's developing control of letter names and forms. If a learner has difficulty naming several letters, you may wish to use the page later in the year so that both you and the child can observe learning development.

Letter Names

Circle the letters named correctly by the student.

You may wish to have the child repeat the task later in the school year if some letters are not named on the initial attempt.

Notes:

Tell me the name of each letter.

h z B e v Y

o i j C I N

A S p c O w

t Q s d T D

m J x b f W

L r U F H q

G K R g a M

E n V y u P

Date: _____   **18**   Name: _____

Consonant and Vowel Sounds

Emerging readers are helped immeasurably by a knowledge of phonics. This does not mean phonetic knowledge, which is terminology used by linguists to describe graphophonic relationships. Readers don't need to know, for instance, what a "digraph" — or even a "short e" — is. There are mature readers, sophisticated readers, who don't know about such things.

Rather, phonics knowledge means knowledge about the correlations between print and sound — which letters and which letter combinations represent which spoken sounds or words. You can assess student use of graphophonic cuing systems as you listen to individual students read, or as you observe student ability to match sound to print in writing. You can also assess learners in direct demonstrations, as this page invites.

To proceed, select one or more sounds to focus on, and jot down the words in the left-hand column. Record if the child repeats a sound (some will not need to) and the letter or sound named by the child.

Use this page as often as necessary to provide a record of an emergent reader's literacy development. On different occasions, you might focus on initial sounds, ending sounds, and middle sounds. If children are able to hear and name vowel sounds, they are showing an increasingly sophisticated ability to use graphophonic cues and an evolving understanding of print.

Consonant and Vowel Sounds

Select a series of words featuring beginning, ending, or middle sounds according to your needs. List the words below.

Note whether the student repeats each sound, and record the vowel or consonant sound named by the student.

Words administered:

- ☐
- ☐
- ☐
- ☐
- ☐
- ☐
- ☐
- ☐
- ☐
- ☐
- ☐
- ☐
- ☐
- ☐
- ☐

Notes:

Tell me what sound you hear at the beginning (*or the middle or the end*) of each word. What letters do you hear?

Student repeats this sound	Names the letter as...
_____	_____
_____	_____
_____	_____
_____	_____
_____	_____
_____	_____
_____	_____
_____	_____
_____	_____
_____	_____
_____	_____
_____	_____
_____	_____
_____	_____
_____	_____
_____	_____
_____	_____
_____	_____

Date: _____

Name: _____

Consonant Combinations

As learners become more sophisticated in their ability to match sounds to letters and words, they may still require help with particular initial or final consonant combinations.

To proceed, select an appropriate series of words, and jot them down in the left-hand column of the page. Record if the child repeats the sounds (some will not need to), and note those named by the child.

Use this page as often as necessary to provide a record of the child's strengths and needs.

Consonant Combinations

Select a series of words according to your needs. List the words below.

Note whether the student repeats the combination, and record the consonant sounds named by the student.

Tell me what sounds you hear at the beginning (*or the end*) of each word. What letters do you hear?

Words administered:

☐
☐
☐
☐
☐
☐
☐
☐
☐
☐
☐
☐
☐
☐
☐
☐

Notes:

Student repeats these consonant sounds	Names the letters as...

Date: _____

20

Name: _____

Diphthongs and Digraphs

The ability to hear and name vowel or vowel-consonant combinations in words demonstrates a sophisticated ability to use graphophonic cues and an evolving familiarity with print.

Use this page to assess a learner's ability to match letter names to sounds. Knowledge about how well a child can make such connections will guide your decisions concerning intervention for particular combinations of letters.

To proceed, select an appropriate series of words, or use those suggested on the page.

Use this page as you require to check on the learner's strengths and needs.

Diphthongs and Digraphs

Select and present the following words, or add your own. Observe whether the student needs support with particular vowels or vowel combinations.

Words administered:

Short "e" sound:
head better said

❏

Long "a" sound:
game rain stay

❏

Long "e" sound:
Pete street eat

❏

Long "i" sound:
pie high smile

❏

Long "o" sound:
spoke goat grow

❏

Long "u" sound:
few true too

❏

The "er" sound:
turn serve bird word

❏

Combinations with "o":
cook loud plough through food soil boy show

❏

Combinations with "a":
claw because farm

❏

Notes:

Story Structure

As students listen to stories that you read aloud, they actively construct meaning. They focus their listening, summon their knowledge of how stories go, and make and confirm predictions.

This page allows them to demonstrate their oral comprehension and their knowledge of sequence and story structure (although it could also be used as a follow-up to students' own reading of a story). Use this page with individuals or with the whole class.

Read to the children any story that has a distinctive beginning, middle, and end, and have them draw pictures illustrating each of the three parts.

In conference, encourage each child to talk about the illustrated scenes and to label the pictures.

Use this page at the beginning and the end of the school year to provide a record of the learner's increasing awareness of story structure.

Story Structure

Draw a picture that shows something from the beginning of the story.

Draw a picture that shows something from the middle of the story.

Draw a picture that shows something from the end of the story.

Understanding Information

Cloze procedure is a tool for assessing a student's ability to use semantic and syntactic cues to predict meaning. This page provides a demonstration of one type of Cloze activity, but how you structure a Cloze passage will depend on your instructional objectives. This passage is offered with the understanding that it will be too difficult for some children, too easy for others. Not simply a test of memory, it invites a variety of responses.

If this piece is appropriate for your students and your purposes, you can use it to assess their ability to process verbal information, as well as their ability to use semantic and syntactic cues.

With the learner, preview both the following text and the Cloze passage to establish a purpose for listening. After listening to the text, the learner can work through the Cloze passage (or you can scribe the student's responses). As he or she does so, observe the strategies used to make sense of the passage. Reread the text as necessary for the student to complete the passage. For more information about Cloze procedure, you may wish to consult Holdaway (1979). Use Cloze activities as you require throughout the school year to support your programming needs.

Sample Text: The Mice and the Cat

The mice once held a meeting to decide what to do about the cat. The cat made their lives miserable. He was always sneaking up among them and eating one of their number.

Though the mice talked for hours, not one of them could think of a solution to the problem. Finally a young mouse spoke up.

"I know what we can do!" he said. "The trouble with the cat is that he is so quiet. We have no warning about when he is coming. So let's get a small bell, put it on a collar, and tie it around the cat's neck. Whenever we hear the bell, we can run for cover."

The other mice were delighted with this idea. They praised the young mouse for his cleverness and wished they had thought of the idea themselves.

But then an old mouse asked, "And which of us will volunteer to approach the cat and tie a bell on him?"

The mice fell silent. Not one of them volunteered to bell the cat.

Moral: Ideas that won't work are not worth anything.

Understanding Information

Establish a purpose for listening by explaining the task to the student and previewing the Cloze passage. Then read the text aloud.

Go over the Cloze passage with the student, and scribe his or her responses. All logical answers are acceptable.

Repeat the reading as often as necessary.

Observe the strategies the student has in place for making sense of the Cloze passage.

Strategies for predicting content:

❏
❏
❏

Notes:

The Mice and the Cat

The characters in this story were not people. They were _____. The mice held a meeting to _____ what to do about the cat. The problem with the cat was that he was so _____ . The mice had no _____ he was coming. They talked for hours, but they could not _____ a solution to the problem.

Finally, a young mouse _____ an idea. The mice would _____ a bell on the cat's collar. Then they could _____ when they heard the cat coming.

The other mice were _____ with the idea. They _____ the young mouse and wished they had thought of the idea themselves. But then an old mouse asked which mouse would _____ to tie a bell on the cat. The mice _____ silent. Not one of them offered to bell the cat.

Date: _____   **23**   Name: _____

Responding to Literature

As children read, they find out about themselves and their relationships with others. They come to see that literature can help them find out about their world — and about places and cultures they will never see. And they delight in the pleasure of a good story.

They begin, as well, to think critically about what they read. They develop preferences for particular authors, genres, or topics. They develop their awareness of literary patterns, techniques, styles, and vocabulary.

We can foster such appreciation of literature by encouraging children to respond to what they read in a variety of ways. This page provides an opportunity for you and the learner to participate in a conversation about a piece of literature.

Use this page at the beginning and the end of the school year so that both you and the child can observe the child's continuing literacy development.

Responding to Literature

Choose a narrative of an appropriate level of difficulty for the student.

Establish a purpose for listening by previewing this page.

After previewing the narrative, read it aloud. Then scribe student responses to the piece, prompting as necessary.

Reread the narrative and repeat the task as often as necessary.

Title of selection:

Notes:

Tell me what happened in the story.

_____

_____

_____

What was your favorite part of the story? Why was that?

_____

_____

_____

Describe your favorite scene in the story.

_____

_____

_____

Tell me about one of the people (*or animals*) in the story.

_____

_____

_____

Tell Me a Story

With beginning writers, the physical (and mental) work of transcribing their thoughts into print often inhibits their actual writing production. This is especially true of students whose fine motor skills lag somewhat. At the same time, beginning writers often focus inordinately on form as they attempt to gain control of and use of print. Thus, if the only records we have of the learner's ideas and imagination are those written by the learner, we often miss an opportunity to appreciate the richness of the child's ability to "compose" mentally.

For this reason, it is useful to have mature language users (older students and parent volunteers) scribe for young writers. Scribing removes the frustration sometimes felt by beginning writers and frees up the generation of material. It gives us a window on children's thinking, especially on their imaginative capacity and ability to generate ideas. Scribing allows us to observe the fluency and organization of their composition and their ability to sequence ideas and shape material so that it has a beginning, middle, and end. We can also pay attention to their ability to use different kinds of sentence patterns and to imitate rhythm or rhyme patterns from literature.

It is instructive for teachers, as well as heartening for learners, to see the quality and amount of print they can generate through a scribe. Students are often encouraged by seeing the written production of their ideas and motivated to increase their ability to do this independently.

Since most children require prior processing time to show their best thinking, give them a day's notice to prepare for telling a story to you or a scribe. Invite them to bring in a photograph or an object, such as a piece of sports equipment or a favorite toy, that has a story they can tell you.

You may wish to use this page more than once during the school year, particularly with children whose ability to compose verbally is greater than their ability to compose in writing.

Tell Me a Story

Give the student a day's notice to prepare for making up a story to tell to a scribe, who will record the story on this page.

Students might bring in a photograph, toy, or other object to talk about.

Observe:

❏ fluency of language use
❏ sequencing of plot/narration
❏ ability to elaborate
❏ beginning
❏ ending
❏ logical structure
❏ use of literary conventions
❏ character description
❏ humor

❏
❏

Notes:

Date: _____

Name: _____

My Talk Checklist

Through talk, students share information, experiences, feelings, and ideas. As they reflect on how they listen and speak, they begin to think about the kinds of talk that are appropriate for particular purposes and audiences, which in turn helps them to speak and respond more effectively. They confirm for themselves that they are good speakers and listeners, but they also think about how they can improve themselves in these areas or broaden their repertoire of oral language skills.

This checklist provides an opportunity for the student to reflect upon personal communication patterns and preferences in the context of the classroom. It also encourages the student to set goals for oral language behavior.

Discuss each statement with the child, and have the child respond. Responses to this checklist will provide a broader picture of each child's views on oral participation in classroom activities. They will also give you a clearer sense of the instructional strategies that are most promising for individual learners.

Present this page early in the school year to provide a reference point against which oral language development can be measured. Then use the page as frequently as necessary to support your reporting schedule — and so that students can observe their increasing oral language confidence and repertoire.

My Talk Checklist

Have the student read and respond to each statement, or read the statements and scribe student responses.

The student can then set personal goals for oral language behavior.

You may wish to have the student revisit this page later in the school year.

Notes:

Think about each of the following statements. Which answer best describes what you do or how you feel?

I like to talk
- ❏ to a partner.
- ❏ in a small group.
- ❏ to the class.

	Often	Some-times	Seldom	Not Yet
I think about what I am going to say before I start to speak.	❏	❏	❏	❏
I like to talk through something I am going to do or write.	❏	❏	❏	❏
I ask questions and join in class discussions.	❏	❏	❏	❏
I listen carefully when others speak.	❏	❏	❏	❏
I am brief and to the point when I speak.	❏	❏	❏	❏
I repeat myself.	❏	❏	❏	❏
I like to read aloud.	❏	❏	❏	❏
I like to take part in skits or plays.	❏	❏	❏	❏
I like to try character voices or accents.	❏	❏	❏	❏
I like to use new words I have learned.	❏	❏	❏	❏
I'm a good speaker and listener.	❏	❏	❏	❏

How I'm going to make myself an even better speaker and listener:

_____

_____

_____

Date: _____   **26**   Name: _____

Listening and Speaking

Research tells us that the learning "basics" are really speaking and thinking, which come developmentally before reading and writing. It also tells us that educators should be concerned about creating opportunities for learners to participate in the world by actively processing and articulating experience, rather than by assuming roles of spectators or passive observers.

Many classroom experiences provide insight into what learners are thinking and how they learn. The questions children pose, the stories they tell, the predictions and connections they make, and the observations they share about their experience are some examples that reflect their thinking.

There are many opportunities in the classroom to assess student talk, which forms the basis for all student interaction and learning. To document such talk formally, you might attach anecdotal notes about student talk to the appropriate portfolio pages. Use this page to synthesize your observations about a learner's ability to use and respond to language.

Use this page after you have had some time to observe the children's oral language performance in different contexts. At the end of the school year, or more frequently if your reporting schedule demands, use the page again to document a child's oral language development.

Listening and Speaking

Complete this page after you have had an opportunity to observe the student's oral language abilities in different contexts.

Check the student's demonstrated abilities, and add any pertinent comments or examples.

Notes:

The student:

In this area the student is

	Strong	Adequate	Weak
Contributes ideas and opinions to discussions.	❑	❑	❑
Makes requests; asks for directions and information.	❑	❑	❑
Shares information, ideas, feelings.	❑	❑	❑
Uses facial and voice expression and gestures.	❑	❑	❑
Can speak in groups of different sizes.	❑	❑	❑
Retells stories.	❑	❑	❑
Uses oral language in a variety of modes.	❑	❑	❑
Indicates enjoyment of language sounds and rhythms.	❑	❑	❑
Listens attentively when stories are read aloud.	❑	❑	❑
Follows verbal directions.	❑	❑	❑
Listens when others speak.	❑	❑	❑
Imitates rhythm and rhyme.	❑	❑	❑

Date: _____ **27** Name: _____

Student Talk

Because speech is both a process and a product of thinking, it is valuable at times for us to focus on students' speaking skills and behaviors, on the quality of their speech. At the same time, we can observe their ability to compose mentally and to share such composition verbally.

Establish a time for the learner to make an oral presentation, and provide time to prepare for the performance. The child might orally present a research report or story he or she has written. Alternatively, the child could talk about a subject of personal interest.

Use this page at the beginning and the end of the school year, and more frequently as your reporting needs dictate.

Student Talk

If possible, base your records on authentic examples of oral language performance in the classroom. Alternatively, have the student tell about something of importance to him or her.

Check the student's demonstrated abilities, and add any pertinent comments or examples.

Notes:

Student Topic: _____

In this area the student is

Strong   Adequate   Weak

The student:

	Strong	Adequate	Weak
Gives details and/or background information.	❏	❏	❏
Identifies main events or points in narration.	❏	❏	❏
Provides information in a logical order.	❏	❏	❏
Responds logically to questions or promptings.	❏	❏	❏
Uses conventional grammar and forms.	❏	❏	❏
Speaks clearly and uses appropriate expression.	❏	❏	❏
Makes eye contact and uses gestures.	❏	❏	❏
Is aware of audience response.	❏	❏	❏
Stays on topic.	❏	❏	❏

Uses when speaking:
- ❏ immature vocabulary
- ❏ adequate vocabulary
- ❏ sophisticated vocabulary

Date: _____

28

Name: _____

Color Words

This page provides an opportunity to observe the learner's familiarity with and knowledge about print — in this case, the ability to read color words. It is also an occasion to assess the child's understanding of color and to observe the child's ability to attend to instructions.

Make available crayons in each of the colors: blue, brown, green, orange, pink, purple, red, and yellow.

Then have the child read the directions and the word under each picture and color each picture accordingly.

In conference, encourage children to talk about how they were able to read the print. Those who are using picture cues may use different colors from those named — ones that are more logical for them.

Use this page as needed with emergent readers.

This task can be used to assess student ability to read color words and follow directions; or it can be used to assess semantic knowledge of color.

The student will need pencils or crayons in the eight colors identified.

Check here if directions were read:

☐ to the student
☐ by the student

Notes:

Color Words

Color each picture with the color named.

blue   pink   brown

red   orange   purple

yellow   green

Date: _____   29   Name: _____

Reading Directions

We know that decoding alone does not constitute reading. As teachers, we want to know how learners understand what they read.

Having children follow a set of simple instructions reveals to us their ability to comprehend and analyze information presented in text and to follow directions.

Use this page as needed with early readers.

Reading Directions

Have the student read and follow the directions.

In the early grades, many children will not be able to complete this page independently.

Notes:

Print the first letter of your name on this line. _____

Place a dot in this circle.

Underline a word that starts with "w."

Circle the last word on this line.

Write your age in the square.

Write the number twelve on the cup.

Write the number four on the bird.

Draw a sun here.

Make a happy face out of this circle.

Show raindrops falling from this cloud.

Following Directions

Tasks involving a series of steps, such as recipes, science experiments, and this page, give us an opportunity to assess a child's ability to comprehend and analyze information presented in text and to follow directions.

To complete the page, children will require semantic knowledge and problem-solving skills, as well as an ability to read.

Use this page as needed with early readers.

Children who are more fluent in their language use might work together to write and follow new directions. One child can follow his or her partner's directions; then the two can switch roles.

Following Directions

Have students read and follow the directions independently.

This task could be used with a small or large group, or with an individual.

Check here if directions were read by:

❏ whole class
❏ small group
❏ individual student

Notes:

Draw a picture by following these directions. After, reread to make sure you have included everything in your picture.

Draw a small house in the middle of the space below.

Draw a tree on the right side of the house.

Draw piles of snow around the house.

Draw a snowperson to the left of the house.

Draw the sun shining.

Draw a path from the house to the bottom of the page.

Draw a mitten beside the path.

Draw a person standing on the path.

Searching for Information

It is important for students to be able to research effectively. The task documented on this page encourages learners to demonstrate their ability to comprehend and analyze information presented in text. It also allows them to show their skimming and scanning skills.

Select a text of an appropriate level of difficulty. The text could be from a newspaper or magazine, or from an expository book. Ask the student to skim or scan the text to locate one or more particular pieces of information.

Observe how the student goes about locating the information and how much time he or she takes.

You may wish to use this page more than once during the school year in order to document the student's ability to approach text in different ways for different purposes.

Searching for Information

Select a piece of text, newspaper page, or article.

Have the student skim or scan to answer a specific question or supply one or more facts or details based on the text.

Observe how the student locates the requested information.

Name of text:

Strategies in place:

☐
☐
☐

Notes:

Description of task(s):

_____

_____

_____

_____

Description of student strategies, behaviors:

_____

_____

_____

_____

Details of student accomplishment:

_____

_____

_____

_____

Date: _____   32   Name: _____

Understanding Print

As we share books with students and observe their attempts to read, we notice and document reading behaviors. In doing so, we observe the strategies children use to make meaning of print, prompting us to create dialog and experiences that will support the development of other strategies.

We have a variety of tools available to us to check on children's understanding of what they have read. Open-ended questions, such as those on this page, allow students to demonstrate their ability to recall information and to sequence, as well as their command of such higher-order skills as making inferences, identifying cause and effect, synthesizing, and drawing conclusions.

Select a text of an appropriate level of difficulty for the student. Preview the text and the questions on this page in order to establish a purpose for reading. Then have the child continue independently and respond to the questions.

Use this page once during each reporting period of the school year to document the child's literacy development, and more often if your schedule demands it.

Understanding Print

Choose a text excerpt of an appropriate level of difficulty.

Establish a purpose for reading by previewing the questions with the student.

Then have the student read the passage independently.

If necessary for fluency, scribe the student's independent responses.

Notes:

What is this story about?

_____

_____

_____

Who are the characters (people or animals) in this story?

_____

_____

_____

What might happen next in this story? Why do you think so?

_____

_____

_____

What was the best part of the story? What made it good?

_____

_____

_____

Date: _____   **33**   Name: _____

Story Mapping

If the students in your class have been working with story maps, you may wish to include one or more examples in the portfolio.

To use this page, have the students read any story that has a distinctive beginning, middle, and end (or, as a check on oral comprehension, read the story to them). Then have them use words, pictures, webs, charts, or graphs — whatever means they are familiar with — to depict the story graphically.

In conference, encourage your learners to retell the story using the visual frames they have created, and have them evaluate how well they have captured the essence of the story in their mapping.

You may wish to use this page early in the school year and then a second time toward the end so that both you and the student can observe an increasing awareness of story structure.

Story Mapping

After your students have read and thoroughly discussed a story with a distinctive beginning, middle, and end, have them map the story to show its main parts.

You might supply a visual organizing frame, such as a circle, boxes, web, or Venn diagram.

This could be done with the class as a whole.

In individual conference, have the student talk about the scenes chosen, and encourage the child to label each picture.

Observe student ability to:

❏ identify beginning, middle, end
❏ trace patterns in plot
❏ recognize cause and effect
❏

Notes:

Think about the story you've just read and talked about. Show the main parts of the story on this page.

Making Inferences

To establish appropriate supports for students in our classrooms, we need information about their ability to comprehend, analyze, and interpret what they read. We also want to know how learners understand what they read. In a practical sense, can they follow print directions? In an interpretive sense, do they see humor? Understand inference? Recognize cause and effect? Distinguish between fact and fantasy? These are aspects of reading ability that go on to distinguish degrees of sophistication within a group of people whom we describe as "knowing how to read."

On this page, have your students make inferences about characters in a story they have read. Because the page is intended as a tool for assessing the student's ability to read and think, scribe responses for them if they need you to do so.

Use this page as often as necessary to support your reporting schedule.

Choose a narrative with strong characterization.

Have the student read the selection and answer the questions.

As this is an instrument for assessing reading and thinking, scribe for students who are unable to write their thoughts here.

Notes:

Making Inferences

What do you learn about the characters in this story?

Character's name: _____

This character is _____

I know this because _____

_____

_____

_____

_____

Character's name: _____

This character is _____

I know this because _____

_____

_____

_____

_____

Identifying Problems

The level of understanding and the clarity with which students articulate story problems reveal a great deal about them as language users. This page provides an opportunity for students to demonstrate their problem-solving skills and their abilities to analyze, make inferences, and clarify.

To proceed, select a piece of literature with a rich plot line, several characters, and several conflicts. Have the students look over the page to establish a purpose for reading. Then have them read the story and identify the chief story problems.

Because the page is intended as a tool for assessing the student's ability to read and think, scribe responses for them if they need you to do so.

Use this page as often as necessary to support your reporting schedule.

Identifying Problems

Select a story excerpt with a complex plot line.

Preview this page with your students, and then have them read the excerpt, stopping before solutions to the problems or conflicts become apparent.

Have the students analyze the problems and pose solutions.

Notes:

Read the story, name the problems, and suggest some solutions to the problems.

In this story, one character with a problem is _____

_____ 's problem is _____

_____

_____

_____

Another character with a problem is _____

_____ 's problem is _____

_____

_____

_____

_____ 's problem could be solved by _____

_____

_____

_____

_____ 's problem could be solved by _____

_____

_____

_____

Responding to Poetry

Children will learn to read and write poetry through exposure to large numbers of poems of different types, rhymed and not, with meter or not, on all the themes that poetry explores.

You foster their responses to poetry by allowing them to find and express their own meaning in a poem, rather than through questions that are geared to recall, interpretation, and searching for the author's purpose.

This page provides a model for some of the kinds of questions that will encourage children to think about poetry.

On a first reading, have the learner listen as you read the poem aloud. Let the child absorb the poem's images, rhyme, and meter. (A child may wish to sit with eyes closed on first reading — but others may emphatically not wish to do so.) Then reread the poem, one stanza at a time, encouraging the child to ask you to pause wherever he or she wishes for reflection or discussion.

Scribe student responses to the poem, either in the course of your conversation about it or after the child has listened to it two or three times.

Throughout the year, have the children respond to poetry in different ways — through writing, art, music, and movement. Collect a variety of materials for the portfolio over the course of the year.

Read this or another poem to the student, inviting individual response to it.

After discussion, scribe student responses.

Notes:

Responding to Poetry
In Fall

Mary Sullivan

In fall the leaves come down.
Some are yellow
and some are brown.
In fall the leaves
come down.

In fall the days
grow cool.
Birds fly south
and we go to school.
In fall the days
grow cool.

In fall the butterflies
are gone.
Mornings are dark
and there's frost on the lawn
in fall.

Do you think the poet likes the fall? What makes you say so?

_____

_____

Close your eyes and think about a fall day. What do you see? Hear? Feel? Smell?

_____

_____

What would you write in a poem about the fall?

_____

_____

_____

Date: _____ **37** Name: _____

My Reading Checklist

Most beginning readers who have had extensive experience with print and story before starting school are light years ahead of those who have not had such experience. Information about this critical "hidden foundation" for learning to read is invaluable to us as we design appropriate support structures for the growth of young readers.

Since we know that "learning how to read" and "becoming a reader" are two different things, we also want to know about the reading patterns of early and emergent readers in order to encourage the development of the "reading habit" in them. Out-of-school reading, family models, and motivation to read are important aspects of this development. As well, it is useful for us to know the interests of our students, the kinds of book they read, the amount of reading they do, and the circumstances that enhance reading for them.

Using this page at the beginning and the end of the school year provides a record of the learner's breadth of experience with literature of various types, preferences, and use of reading strategies.

My Reading Checklist

Discuss or read the statements, and record the student's responses and comments.

Notes:

	Often	Some-times	Hardly Ever	Not Yet
I read well.				
I read stories.				
I read poems.				
I read directions.				
I read to find out about things.				
I like to read or investigate books with a partner.				
I like to read on my own.				
I like to read to the class.				
I like to read at home.				
I read magazines.				
I read parts of the newspaper.				
I choose books by my favorite author.				
I choose books by my favorite illustrator.				
I like to talk about books with my friends.				
I learn new words when I read.				
I try to figure out what a book is about before I start reading.				
I use pictures and diagrams to help me understand a book.				

Date: _____ **38** Name: _____

Thoughts About Reading

Information about a learner's attitudes toward and preferences in reading helps us to provide support and context for the child's growth as a reader. As we share books with learners and observe their attempts to read, we notice and document their reading behaviors. After determining which strategies children use to make meaning of print, we can create dialog and experiences that will support the development of other strategies. In this way, we can broaden the learner's repertoire of strategies and strengthen the perception of self as reader.

If, for instance, we see the reader attacking sounds initially without seeming to notice pictures or show an interest in a text in a global way, we know that we can help by drawing attention to the possible subject of the text and opening up the student's knowledge of the content area.

Students are helped by a heightened awareness of their habits and preferences, and this page encourages reflection and self-assessment.

Using this page at the beginning and the end of the school year provides a record of the learner's breadth of experience with literature of various types, preferences, and use of reading strategies.

Discuss or read the statements, and record the student's responses and comments.

Notes:

Thoughts About Reading

My favorite books are _____

_____

_____

My favorite author is _____

because _____

_____

_____

When I have trouble reading, I _____

_____

_____

What I want to improve in my reading: _____

_____

_____

How I can become a better reader: _____

_____

_____

Date: _____   **39**   Name: _____

About Literature

This page fosters reflection on genre and helps learners synthesize their expanding knowledge of the language of literacy. It also encourages them to think about how they make meaning from text.

To begin, select several pieces of writing that the children are familiar with. Some possibilities include a poem, a picture book, a magazine article, a cartoon, a recipe, a set of directions, a letter, a newspaper article, an advertisement, a shopping list, and a cereal box.

Invite the children to name each type of writing and talk about its purpose(s). Let them speculate on the content of each piece, and encourage them to talk about how they made their predictions. Note their responses, and summarize your observations on this page.

Begin to develop with the children a common vocabulary of literary expression, using with them such terms as *author*, *character*, *plot*, and *setting*.

Use this page as frequently as your programming and reporting needs dictate.

About Literature

Collect and present several samples of different kinds of writing.

Read the samples with the student, encouraging the child to discuss and identify each type of writing and its purpose. In the course of your conversation, elicit such terms as *author*, *character*, and *dedication*.

Have the student speculate on the content of each piece, and record the predictions. Have the student reflect on how the predictions were made.

Notes:

The student:

can distinguish fiction from non-fiction.

_____

can identify characters in a narrative and make inferences about character feelings and motivations.

_____

can identify the purpose of a piece of writing.

_____

is able to use the following literary terms:

_____

_____

_____

has the following strategies in place to predict content:

_____

_____

_____

needs support to develop the following learning strategies:

_____

_____

_____

Date: _____   Name: _____

Selected Work

When learners select work for inclusion in their portfolios, they demonstrate their critical appreciation of their work. In discussing their choices, they reveal their criteria for evaluation and provide evidence of their self-concept as writers.

One way in which portfolios differ from writing folders is that the materials preserved in them are retained for as long as the child remains in school to provide a permanent record of literacy development. To help ensure that a child selects his or her best work, photocopy the work for the portfolio and let the child keep or display the original.

Have the child select one piece of work for the portfolio during each reporting period — and more if space permits.

Have the student select a piece of work for inclusion in the portfolio. If possible, photocopy the work and let the child retain the original.

Scribe the child's assessment of the work.

Add relevant background information and your observations about the piece.

Notes:

Selected Work

I chose this piece because:

_____

_____

_____

_____

_____

_____

Where I got my ideas for this piece of writing:

_____

_____

_____

_____

_____

_____

Date: _____ **41** Name: _____

Information Writing

Personal narratives are the most common form of writing for children in the primary grades. Yet fluent language users write for many purposes — among others, to describe, to report, to explain, and to explore.

This page is a prompt for collecting some of these other kinds of texts. It also provides an opportunity for assessment of student ability to:

- establish a purpose for writing and identify an audience
- use the library or on-line databases to locate information
- structure material logically with a beginning, middle, and end
- experiment with a variety of forms for presenting expository material
- acknowledge sources completely and accurately
- work with an editor to revise the writing
- integrate visuals with written work

In individual conference, discuss a piece of exposition the student has written, and then invite the student to evaluate both the product and the process that led to it.

Use this page to support your classroom needs and reporting schedules.

Information Writing

In individual conference, discuss a piece of exposition that the student has written, and have the student evaluate the work.

Also discuss research strategies and how to structure expository text.

Observe:

- ☐ evidence of careful research
- ☐ how research is integrated in the text
- ☐ text structure
- ☐ coherence and readability of the text
- ☐ whether sources are properly acknowledged
- ☐

Research strategies in place:

- ☐
- ☐
- ☐

Notes:

My topic is: _____

	YES	NOT YET
I research my topic thoroughly.	☐	☐
I write down my sources.	☐	☐
I make good notes.	☐	☐
I write the information I find in my own words.	☐	☐
I copy quotations carefully.	☐	☐
I organize my work so that it has a good beginning, middle, and end.	☐	☐

What I learned:

_____

_____

_____

_____

What I want to do better the next time:

_____

_____

_____

_____

Date: _____ **42** Name: _____

Writing a Sequel

The connections that children make between their reading and their writing reveal how they have understood what they have read, their ability to make inferences, their imaginative capacity, and their ability to project.

As they write a sequel, they show their ability to imitate the author's style and language patterns and their ability to think critically about a piece of literature. They also demonstrate that they can compose written material for a particular purpose and audience.

Use this page to support your classroom needs and reporting schedules.

Have the student draft a sequel for a story. You may wish to scribe for students whose fine motor skills lag.

Observe:

❑ whether narrative is believable
❑ whether characters are lifelike
❑ whether dialog is realistic
❑ clarity of sequence of events
❑ consistency of point of view
❑ whether sequence is logical
❑ interesting beginning; satisfying conclusion
❑ sensitivity to language patterns, characters, and plot of original text
❑ variety in sentence structures
❑ word choice and variety
❑ whether verb tense is consistent
❑ spelling of common words
❑ spelling of unfamiliar words
❑ use of punctuation
❑ amount of material generated
❑

Notes:

Pick a story you know well and extend it. Use more pages if you need to.

_____

_____

_____

_____

_____

_____

_____

_____

_____

_____

_____

_____

_____

_____

Date: _____ **43** Name: _____

About Writing

What learners tell us about writing and about themselves as writers can give us vital clues regarding the support and intervention strategies that will help ease frustration or foster literacy development. Reflection on their work also brings insight to learners as they attempt to articulate feelings about their work.

Reflection may be prompted through dialog in interviews, as some writers have to "hear what they say to know what they mean." This page is intended as a stimulus for such reflection. It encourages learners to reflect on how they begin to write and on their writing strategies.

If a child is at a very early stage of writing development, the discussion might take a form such as the following:

Let's say a visitor to our classroom doesn't know how to write. What would you tell the visitor about writing? If you were to show the visitor how to write, what would you do?

Using this page at the beginning and the end of the school year (and more frequently, if necessary, for reporting purposes) will enable both you and the child to observe the child's development and developing self-concept as a writer.

In individual conference, read the questions and scribe the student's responses.

Notes:

About Writing

Why do people write?

_____

_____

_____

What do you like best about writing?

_____

_____

_____

What do you like to write about?

_____

_____

_____

How do you start to write a story or poem?

_____

_____

_____

_____

Date: _____ 44 Name: _____

About Revising

Children are greatly assisted in their writing if they think about the "why" of what they are doing, along with the "what."

To proceed, have the learner select a piece of writing that has been or is being revised. Invite discussion of the process of revision.

Use this page at the beginning and the end of the school year, and more frequently, if necessary, for reporting purposes.

About Revising

In conference, discuss a piece of writing that the child is revising.

Have the child reflect on the process of revision. Scribe the student's responses.

Notes:

How do you decide you need to change something in your work?

_____

_____

_____

How do you help your classmates with their writing?

_____

_____

_____

What do you do if you don't know how to spell a word?

_____

_____

_____

How do you check your punctuation marks?

_____

_____

_____

Date: _____ **45** Name: _____

Writing and Editing

Writing is a process that involves developing ideas into more and more coherent written form. This page provides an opportunity for you to capture and discuss children's perception of writing as a process and some of the strategies they are using to revise and edit their work. It also provides to both you and the student evidence of growth in critical thinking abilities.

To begin, invite the learner to tell you about something of importance to him or her. As the child speaks, create three to five sentences based on what the child has said. Read the sentences back to the child for transcription.

Then have the learner read aloud what has been written and talk about how the writing could be made better. Which additional details could be included, and which could be omitted? Which descriptive words might be added? Help the child make the revisions in colored pencil or ink.

When the child is satisfied with the content of the writing, encourage a look at its mechanics. What words or letters are missing? Are capitalization and punctuation correct? Again, help the child to revise. If a child is uncertain of the spelling of a particular word, encourage him or her to underline it and speculate on how else the word might be spelled.

Use this page to support your classroom needs and reporting schedules.

Writing and Editing

Create three to five sentences based on a narrative a student relates to you. Reread the sentences aloud for the student to transcribe.

Then have the student reread the sentences. Encourage reflection on how the writing might be improved. Help the child to make some revisions to the text. Invite revision of content and structure, as well as mechanics.

Observe ability to:

- ❑ revise for clarity
- ❑ revise for improved legibility
- ❑ use conventional spellings
- ❑ use conventional punctuation
- ❑

Notes:

Date: _____

Name: _____

My Writing Checklist

To provide appropriate supports for learners, we need information about their attitudes toward writing and toward themselves as writers.

This page provides an opportunity for such assessment. In reflecting on their practices and habits, students become aware of their strengths and are supported in their writing. They feel more ownership for their learning and more control over their movement toward their own learning goals.

With the learner, review published pieces of writing or pieces of writing in the writing folder. After explaining this page, initiate a conversation about writing: what it means to be a writer, the purposes of writing, the student's attitude toward writing, what he or she does well. Record responses to each statement.

Plan on using this page during each reporting period of the school year.

My Writing Checklist

Review with the student pieces of writing from his or her writing folder.

Read the statements to the student, and encourage reflection.

Notes:

	Most of the time	Some-times	Hardly Ever	Not Yet
I write well.				
I like to write.				
I write so that other people can read what I write.				
I have good ideas for writing.				
I research before I write.				
It helps me to write if I draw a picture first.				
I use capital letters when I write.				
I make up spellings when I don't know the words.				
I have good beginnings and endings in my stories.				
I know how to use periods, commas, question marks, and exclamation marks.				
I use the dictionary and the thesaurus.				
I like to draw a picture after I write.				
I like to share my work with others.				
I use the computer for writing.				

Date: _____ 47 Name: _____

Before I Write

This page invites learners to focus on their prewriting strategies and practices. As they identify and evaluate themselves as practitioners of the craft of writing, they become more aware of different areas of development. They also become familiar with how they may increase their repertoire of prewriting strategies.

Have students work through this checklist either in conference with you or independently.

Use this page as often as necessary to provide a record of a child's development as a writer.

Before I Write

Gather several pieces of the student's in-process work.

Read the statements with the student, and invite self-assessment. Encourage the student to refer to his or her work as necessary to respond.

Notes:

Think about the writing you have done at school or at home. Which of the following do you do before you write?

	Often	Some-times	Seldom	Not Usually
I think about my topic a lot before I write anything.	❑	❑	❑	❑
I think about why I'm writing.	❑	❑	❑	❑
I think about who I'm writing for.	❑	❑	❑	❑
I talk to someone about my ideas for writing.	❑	❑	❑	❑
I imagine the situation I am writing about.	❑	❑	❑	❑
I look at books or pictures to get ideas.	❑	❑	❑	❑
I sketch or map or web what I am thinking about.	❑	❑	❑	❑
I write about things that interest me.	❑	❑	❑	❑
I act out what I'm going to write about.	❑	❑	❑	❑
I ask questions.	❑	❑	❑	❑
I write and write and write until I know what I want to say.	❑	❑	❑	❑
I think about different ways of beginning my piece.	❑	❑	❑	❑
I think about different ways of ending my piece.	❑	❑	❑	❑
I jot down words and phrases.	❑	❑	❑	❑
I note writing I like and imitate it in my work.	❑	❑	❑	❑

Date: _____   48   Name: _____

While I'm Writing

This page invites learners to focus on their drafting strategies and practices. As they identify and evaluate themselves as practitioners of the craft of writing, they become more aware of different areas of development. They also become familiar with how they may increase their repertoire of drafting strategies.

Have students work through this checklist either in conference with you or independently.

Use this page as often as necessary to provide a record of a child's development as a writer.

While I'm Writing

Gather several pieces of the student's in-process work.

Read the statements with the student, and invite self-assessment. Encourage the student to refer to his or her work as necessary to respond.

Notes:

Think about the writing you have done at school or at home. Which of the following do you while you are writing?

	Often	Some-times	Seldom	Not Usually
I organize myself before I write.	☐	☐	☐	☐
I write as much as I can think of without stopping.	☐	☐	☐	☐
I write slowly and think about each word before I put it down.	☐	☐	☐	☐
I spell the best I can and keep writing.	☐	☐	☐	☐
I look words up in the dictionary to make sure they're right the first time.	☐	☐	☐	☐
I know what I'm going to say before I start to write.	☐	☐	☐	☐
I figure out what I'm writing about while I'm writing.	☐	☐	☐	☐
I finish a piece of writing before I start a new one.	☐	☐	☐	☐
I have several piece of writing in my folder and I work on them when I'm ready.	☐	☐	☐	☐
My writing is right the first time.	☐	☐	☐	☐
I write several drafts before I'm happy with my writing.	☐	☐	☐	☐
If I get stuck in my writing, I reread my work and look for something new to say.	☐	☐	☐	☐
If I get stuck in my writing, I try to picture more clearly the people, places, or things I'm writing about.	☐	☐	☐	☐
If I get stuck in my writing, I talk over my piece with a classmate.	☐	☐	☐	☐
If I get stuck in my writing, I find a different piece of writing and work on it instead.	☐	☐	☐	☐

Date: _____

Name: _____

Changing My Work

As writers revise, they shape and organize material through a writing process that moves the writing toward increased sophistication and precision. In receiving responses to the content of their work, they are encouraged to express their ideas with increasing correctness and refinement. When we focus on the use of interesting vocabulary, the provision of descriptive detail, the use of diverse sentence patterns, and the presence of figurative language or humor, we encourage students to extend their writing skills — and to look for and appreciate these in the writing of others.

This page invites learners to focus on their revision strategies and practices. As they identify and evaluate themselves as practitioners of the craft of writing, they become more aware of different areas of development. They also become familiar with how they may increase their repertoire of revision strategies.

Have students work through the checklist either in conference with you or independently.

Use this page as often as necessary to provide a record of a child's development as a writer.

Changing My Work

Gather several pieces of the student's in-process work.

Read the statements with the student, and invite self-assessment. Encourage the student to refer to his or her work as necessary to respond.

Notes:

Think about the writing you have done at school or at home. Which of the following do you do after you've finished your first draft?

	Often	Some-times	Seldom	Not Usually
I reread my draft to make sure it says what I want it to say.	☐	☐	☐	☐
I ask others to look at my work and suggest changes.	☐	☐	☐	☐
I read my work to others.	☐	☐	☐	☐
I check to make sure I haven't said too much.	☐	☐	☐	☐
I check to make sure I've said enough.	☐	☐	☐	☐
I check to make sure I've said things in the clearest order.	☐	☐	☐	☐
I change the order of details.	☐	☐	☐	☐
I cross things out.	☐	☐	☐	☐
I add ideas.	☐	☐	☐	☐
I use arrows to move things around or add new material.	☐	☐	☐	☐
I combine sentences or separate them.	☐	☐	☐	☐
I change words.	☐	☐	☐	☐
I check my spelling and my punctuation.	☐	☐	☐	☐
I check my capital letters.	☐	☐	☐	☐
I use pictures to make my writing clearer.	☐	☐	☐	☐
I rewrite a good copy so that others can read it.	☐	☐	☐	☐
I share my work with others.	☐	☐	☐	☐
I keep a copy of my work.	☐	☐	☐	☐

Date: _____   **50**   Name: _____

How I Spell

Information about the student's awareness of and interest in words tells us something about his or her spelling aptitude. As we assess individual needs and plan classroom instruction, it is important for us to know what strategies are in place for remembering, for figuring out, and for verifying spelling.

This checklist encourages the student to share some of that information with us.

Use this page during each reporting period of the school year, or more frequently as you need to.

Read the statements with the student and invite self-assessment.

The student can then set personal goals for spelling improvement.

Notes:

How I Spell

Check all of the responses that describe your approach to spelling and to new words.

When I'm writing and I come to a word I don't know how to spell...

☐ I write the word the first way that comes into my head, and I keep going.

☐ I try to sound out the word, and if it looks right I keep writing.

☐ I find it hard to go on writing until I am sure of the spelling.

☐ I look around the room and at books and word lists trying to find the word.

☐ I ask someone how to spell it.

☐ I try to look it up in the dictionary.

☐ I spell it like a similar word that I know how to spell.

☐ I make sure I have the right spelling of all the words before I do my final draft.

When I'm reading...

☐ I notice the spelling of words.

☐ I notice when a word is spelled in a way I don't expect.

☐ I think of a way to remember a new word or spelling.

In general...

☐ I find words and letter combinations interesting.

☐ I find it's easy to picture words and to remember the order of letters.

What I would like to improve in my spelling:

_____

_____

How I could do this:

_____

_____

Date: _____ **51** Name: _____

Dictation

The ability to transcribe language is independent of the ability to compose written language — that is, to generate and organize ideas for writing. If we can separate the two, we can respond to a learner's growing control over language mechanics and conventions with reduced fear of inhibiting the child's confidence in his or her writing ability. This is because students have no part in composing the selection they transcribe.

Transcription allows us to observe the sight words and letter combinations that learners have in their spelling repertoires. Syntactic awareness becomes evident as students use capital letters and punctuation in their transcriptions.

All of the student writing gathered in the portfolio provides information about the mechanics of student writing, but it is important when dealing with such student-generated writing to focus primarily on content and organization.

To proceed with a dictation, select a paragraph of appropriate difficulty and read it aloud for the student to transcribe, rereading the paragraph as often as necessary.

Restrict your comments on the transcription to the left margin of the page.

As students repeat the task throughout the year, they will be able to observe their expanding knowledge of language conventions.

Use this page as often as necessary to provide a record of a child's ability to transcribe.

Dictation

Choose a passage of an appropriate level of difficulty.

Read the passage to an individual or to a small group. Reread as many times as each student requires.

You will want to restrict your comments on the dictation to this margin.

Check here if administered:

❏ in small group
❏ to individual

The student:

❏ spells most words in a recognizable form
❏ makes changes to work
❏ prints legibly
❏ spaces words consistently
❏ uses capital letters
❏ uses final punctuation
❏

Spelling strategies in place:

❏
❏
❏

Notes:

My dictation:

_____

_____

_____

_____

_____

_____

_____

_____

_____

_____

_____

_____

_____

_____

Date: _____ **52** Name: _____

Best Printing or Writing

One important aspect of writing lies in being able to share work with others. For this to occur, spelling must approach conventional forms and handwriting should be legible.

As children learn to read and write, their growth in one area furthers their development in the other. Once students recognize a letter in reading, for example, they may soon also be able to visualize and form the letter in writing. As teachers, we are interested in providing opportunity and motivation for learners to gain the kinesthetic skills to form recognizable letters.

You can assess ability to form letters in finished pieces of work that children generate. You can also assess through direct demonstrations. This page provides for such a demonstration of fine motor control.

Using this page, you will be able to see what young writers can do and the kinds of skills and knowledge they still need to acquire. Encourage children to demonstrate their very best printing or handwriting and to take the time to ensure they have done their best.

Use this page as often as necessary to provide a record of a child's ability to transcribe.

The student prints or writes the sentences, taking as much time as needed.

Notes:

Best Printing or Writing

Here is a sample of my best printing or writing.

I am a good writer. If my writing is clear, other people can read it.

_____

_____

_____

_____

_____

_____

_____

_____

_____

_____

My Handwriting Checklist

As they assess their printing or handwriting, children develop their critical thinking skills and reveal their perceptions of themselves as writers. Help them to see that conventional written forms allow others to share their written work.

Use this page as often as necessary to provide a record of a child's perception of his or her ability to transcribe.

My Handwriting Checklist

Have the student look through the portfolio and comment on the presentation of finished pieces.

Then have him or her focus specifically on handwriting, using this checklist as a reference for self-assessment.

Notes:

Printing

YES • NOT YET

I leave the same amount of space between letters. ☐ ☐

I leave the same amount of space between words. ☐ ☐

All my letters face the right way. ☐ ☐

I close round letters completely. ☐ ☐

I make my letters even sizes. ☐ ☐

My letters sit on the line evenly. ☐ ☐

Writing

I form most of the letters well. ☐ ☐

My writing sits on the line. ☐ ☐

My writing all slants in one direction. ☐ ☐

I write almost as fast as I print. ☐ ☐

How I can improve my handwriting:

_____

_____

_____

Date: _____ **54** Name: _____

At Year-End

To bring the year to a close, try to capture student and family views on how learning has progressed.

#	Page	Date	Date
55	Interview		
56	A Final Note from Home		
57	This Year I Grew		

Collect samples and examples for comparison with the baseline work gathered at the beginning of the year.

Put the final brushstrokes on the literacy portrait that has been developing during the year by revisiting pages such as the following.

Finally, gather any other pieces you require for reporting purposes.

Other Works for Assessment	Date

Interview

Interviews are one way to gain information about a learner and his or her self-concept as a member of the learning community. As well, interviews encourage students to present themselves as successful learners and doers.

An end-of-year interview provides closure on the school year. It encourages learners to reflect on their experiences at school and to evaluate their performance against previous personal performance and against the performance of others. It also helps them think about new learning goals for the next school year.

Interview

In a conversation with the student, elicit and record the information on the page.

Notes:

What I like about myself is _____

_____

_____

One of the best things about school this year was _____

_____

_____

Something I am getting better at is _____

_____

_____

Next year at school, I would like to learn to _____

_____

_____

_____

I could learn to do this by _____

_____

_____

_____

A Final Note from Home

This page gives families an opportunity to think about their child's learning gains over the course of the school year. The page invites reflection on the child's accomplishments during the year and on the challenges faced.

The comments on this page will be useful to the child's educators in the new school year, but they will also point to particular strengths of your portfolio program — and to possible ways in which the program might be further improved.

A Final Note from Home

Your comments and observations will be kept in your child's learning portfolio. They will be useful to your child's teacher next year.

Changes you saw in your child this year: _____

_____

_____

Your child's skills and accomplishments this year: _____

_____

_____

What your child enjoyed about the school year: _____

_____

_____

What your child found challenging during the school year: _____

_____

_____

Concerns you have about your child's experiences during the school year: _____

_____

_____

_____

Other comments: _____

_____

_____

_____

Date: _____ 56 Name: _____

This Year I Grew

This page provides an opportunity to discuss and celebrate what the student learned during the school year. Your conversation can reveal much about the student's self-perception as a learner.

Have the student go through the portfolio, comparing early demonstrations with later ones and commenting on learning growth.

Make a note of the observations.

This Year I Grew

Encourage the student to look through the portfolio. Record the child's perceptions of personal growth as a learner.

Notes:

What do you feel really good about learning this year?

_____

_____

_____

In what ways are you a better reader than you were before?

_____

_____

_____

In what ways are you a better writer than you were before?

_____

_____

_____

In what ways are you a better worker than you were before?

_____

_____

In what ways are you a better thinker than you were before?

_____

_____

_____

What things do you want to find out about next year?

_____

_____

How will you find out about these things?

_____

_____

Date: _____   **57**   Name: _____